Who Am I?
This Is Who I Am
A Journey of Self-Discovery

Julie Marshall

BALBOA.
PRESS

A DIVISION OF HAY HOUSE

Balboa Press books may be ordered through booksellers or by contacting:

Balboa Press
A Division of Hay House
1663 Liberty Drive
Bloomington, IN 47403
www.balboapress.com.au
1 (877) 407-4847

Because of the dynamic nature of the Internet, any web addresses or links contained in this book may have changed since publication and may no longer be valid. The views expressed in this work are solely those of the author and do not necessarily reflect the views of the publisher, and the publisher hereby disclaims any responsibility for them.

The author of this book does not dispense medical advice or prescribe the use of any technique as a form of treatment for physical, emotional, or medical problems without the advice of a physician, either directly or indirectly. The intent of the author is only to offer information of a general nature to help you in your quest for emotional and spiritual well-being. In the event you use any of the information in this book for yourself, which is your constitutional right, the author and the publisher assume no responsibility for your actions.

Any people depicted in stock imagery provided by Getty Images are models,
and such images are being used for illustrative purposes only.
Certain stock imagery © Getty Images.

Print information available on the last page.

ISBN: 978-1-5043-1514-2 (sc)
ISBN: 978-1-5043-1515-9 (e)

Balboa Press rev. date: 10/08/2018

With love and gratitude to our families; past, present and future. We are all intertwined.

Who Am I? is a book created to act as a tool that will guide the reader's journey of self-discovery. It has been designed to encourage and develop individual and personal thoughts, values, and experiences. It includes key words and phrases to prompt conversations and self-reflection, each with space to write and/or sketch responses.

Readers should take all the time they need with their responses, perhaps taking the book on holiday or keeping it as a journal. I would also suggest they revisit it every so often to reflect or edit their thoughts. Readers should not be worried about the quality of sketching, as stick figures and outlines will serve visual purpose; the book's focus is bringing forward thoughts and visualizations, not creating a work of art.

Introduction

I have read many books on how to find myself, my soul, and my meaning of life. But these publications tended to reflect another person's ideas, personalities, experiences, and thoughts rather than my own. While they were somewhat inspiring, I was eventually left with the feeling that something was still missing and that there was so much more to who *I am* and what *I* believe.

So I started thinking, doodling, and jotting down my thoughts, ideas, beliefs, and experiences. I began to see the real me emerging from the pencil and the pages in front of me, and to my surprise I started to feel stronger, more confident, and more complete—and definitely happier.

Friends and family close to me noticed the mental, physical, emotional, and spiritual changes I was experiencing. I began to glow with contentment and peace. They asked me to share my deep and private secret of self-discovery, which I will now share with you.

This book is designed to help you to remember who you are or else discover who you are for the first time. You could also use it to find out about someone else, someone you love, such as a partner or a relative.

Your family, ancestors, friends, experiences, and choices all mix together with your environment to create the beautiful tapestry that is you. Wouldn't it be precious to be able to read about the thoughts and experiences of one of your grandparents? Perhaps you would find a deep ancestral connection or better understand why you *tick* like you do.

Embrace this personal journey of self-discovery. Be open, honest, patient, and kind with yourself. You may choose to share your experience with someone you love, or you may prefer to keep it private. Take as long as you need; consider using pencil and even coloured pencils to add texture. You might want to start just by doodling or jotting words that come to you; then over time, as you feel more comfortable and confident, fill in the spaces between the dots and words until you see yourself emerge.

Did you know that unconsciously you are continually steering yourself through your life? Therefore, once you rediscover yourself, you can reset your endeavours and your dreams.

Your own personal universe should fit you like a glove, full of harmony and genuine contentment. Be true to yourself, and be happy.

Who Are You?

When did you stop being you? When did you last feel really content with yourself? What happened? Was it over time, or was there a defining situation or moment? As life unfolds, people come and go; situations and environments enter and leave your life. Sometimes, you have to rediscover yourself or even reinvent your entire universe—for example, when someone close to you dies or leaves you.

Or perhaps, slowly and over time, changes occurred in and around you that were so subtle you didn't even notice until you were lost. It's important to continually audit yourself to keep abreast of life and its changes in order to stay true to who you are and where you belong.

Stop for just a moment, close your eyes, and take a quick look into your soul. Are you really content?

Now, briefly reflect on those five *Ws* and the *H* you learnt at school. *Who* are you, *what* are you doing, *when* did things change, *where* are you (going), *why* are you here or there, and *how* can you steer your current environment or situation to feel more comfortable and compatible with yourself?

Look after your soul, and remember that it's OK to respectfully *call out* a person or a situation that makes you feel uncomfortable or compromised. Let people know how they make you feel. Life can be unpredictable, and every now and then you might be thrown a curve ball, so you need to be as prepared as possible.

Remember Forrest Gump and "life is like a box of chocolates"? Well, my grandfather had a similar analogy. He would say that each day you wake up with a different hand of cards dealt, but you should always play your hand to the best of your ability. Some days are an easy win (you feel great), but other days might be more of a challenge to survive. However, if you stay true to yourself and have confidence in yourself, you will feel content and satisfied that you did your best and that everything will be OK.

The following pages contain titles and subject headings to prompt your memories and thoughts. The titles listed serve as a guide to help you question, remember, and discover yourself. By adding your own wise, thoughtful, heartfelt, and responsive words and illustrations to these subjects, you will create a visual narrative that will reveal who you are. You will realise your values, your virtues, your needs, and your personality. *Who you are* will develop as you begin to explore what you believe, what you feel, and what you want.

So take a deep breath and relax as you begin your odyssey. I'm sure you will cry (with sad and happy thoughts), and you will laugh; however, your journey will be inspiring.

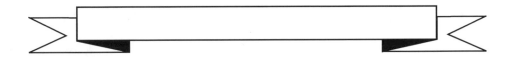

This is who I am.

My name is _____ and I was born in

_____ on _____.

As I journey through life, many people come and go. I also experience many environments and circumstances. My soul looks to itself to find contentment and confidence to remind me who I am and where I belong.

I think.

I feel.

I believe.

I remember.

I need.

I like.

I do.

I have.

I know.

I see.

I understand.

I am.

Part 1

Childhood Memories

❖ My parents

❖ My siblings

_____

_____

_____

_____

_____

_____

_____

_____

_____

_____

_____

_____

❖ Favourite toys or games

_____

_____

_____

_____

_____

_____

_____

_____

_____

_____

_____

_____

_____

_____

_____

_____

_____

_____

_____

_____

_____

_____

_____

❖ Activities or games I enjoyed

_____

_____

_____

_____

_____

_____

_____

_____

_____

_____

_____

❖ Kindergarten or early school

_____

_____

_____

_____

_____

_____

_____

_____

_____

_____

_____

_____

_____

_____

_____

_____

_____

_____

_____

_____

_____

_____

_____

_____

_____

❖ Other memories or thoughts

_____

_____

_____

_____

_____

_____

_____

_____

_____

_____

art 2

Teenage and Early Adult Development

❖ Discovering love or sex

_____

_____

_____

_____

_____

_____

_____

_____

_____

_____

_____

_____

❖ Favourite hobby or subject

❖ Future dreams

_____

_____

_____

_____

_____

_____

_____

_____

_____

_____

_____

_____

❖ Idols or people I admired

❖ First car

❖ Dislikes

❖ Favourite place

_____

_____

_____

_____

_____

_____

_____

_____

_____

_____

_____

_____

❖ Other memories or thoughts

Part 3

Adult Life, Values, and Experiences

❖ Marriage or partners

_____

_____

_____

_____

_____

_____

_____

_____

_____

_____

_____

_____

❖ Travel

❖ Houses I lived in

_____

_____

_____

_____

_____

_____

_____

_____

_____

_____

_____

_____

❖ Favourite season

❖ Spirituality

❖ My beliefs about love

❖ People I love

_____

_____

_____

_____

_____

_____

_____

_____

_____

_____

_____

_____

_____

❖ People or personalities I like or admire

_____

_____

_____

_____

_____

_____

_____

_____

_____

_____

_____

❖ People I avoid

_____

_____

_____

_____

_____

_____

_____

_____

_____

_____

_____

_____

❖ Food likes and dislikes

❖ My favourite colour and number and my reasons

_____

_____

_____

_____

_____

_____

_____

_____

_____

_____

❖ Movie(s) I like and my reasons

_____

_____

_____

_____

_____

_____

_____

_____

_____

_____

❖ Book(s) I like and my reasons

❖ My virtues

❖ Values and ethics

❖ Other memories or thoughts

_____

_____

_____

_____

_____

_____

_____

_____

_____

_____

_____

art 4

Reflections and Thoughts for Conversation

❖ What are my thoughts on death and life after death?

_____

_____

_____

_____

_____

_____

_____

_____

_____

_____

❖ How do I want to be remembered?

_____

_____

_____

_____

_____

_____

_____

_____

_____

_____

_____

❖ What T-junctions have I encountered in my life?

_____

_____

_____

_____

_____

_____

_____

_____

_____

_____

❖ Do I have any regrets?

_____

_____

_____

_____

_____

_____

_____

_____

_____

_____

_____

❖ What is my favourite animal, and why?

_____

_____

_____

_____

_____

_____

_____

_____

_____

_____

❖ What do I like about myself?

_____

_____

_____

_____

_____

_____

_____

_____

_____

_____

_____

❖ What would I change about myself? Why? How?

_____

_____

_____

_____

_____

_____

_____

_____

_____

_____

❖ What are my best qualities?

❖ What qualities do I have that I dislike? For example, am I oversensitive?

_____

_____

_____

_____

_____

_____

_____

_____

_____

_____

❖ What is my favourite environment or happy place (beach, mountains, etc.)?

_____

_____

_____

_____

_____

_____

_____

_____

_____

_____

❖ Why is this my favourite environment?

_____

_____

_____

_____

_____

_____

_____

_____

_____

_____

❖ What type of home makes me feel happy?

_____

_____

_____

_____

_____

_____

_____

_____

_____

_____

_____

❖ What about life do I find confusing?

_____

_____

_____

_____

_____

_____

_____

_____

_____

_____

_____

❖ What career would I love to have or have had?

_____

_____

_____

_____

_____

_____

_____

_____

_____

_____

❖ What characteristics would my ideal partner have?

_____

_____

_____

_____

_____

_____

_____

_____

_____

_____

_____

❖ What qualities do I admire in others?

_____

_____

_____

_____

_____

_____

_____

_____

_____

_____

❖ Whom do I admire?

_____

_____

_____

_____

_____

_____

_____

_____

_____

_____

_____

❖ What type of people do I like, dislike, or need around me?

_____

_____

_____

_____

_____

_____

_____

_____

_____

_____

❖ What makes me sad?

❖ What makes me happy?

❄ What am I grateful for?

_____

_____

_____

_____

_____

_____

_____

_____

_____

_____

_____

❖ What are my thoughts on politics?

_____

_____

_____

_____

_____

_____

_____

_____

_____

_____

_____

_____

❖ I am the product of all my ancestors before me; what are my thoughts about them?

_____

_____

_____

_____

_____

_____

_____

_____

_____

❖ If I could travel in space or time, where would I go, and whom would I meet?

❖ What does my soul say to my body?

_____

_____

_____

_____

_____

_____

_____

_____

_____

_____

_____

❖ What does my body say to my soul?

Self-Acknowledgement, Visualisation, and Gratitude

I am unique, and I have pride in who I am.

I am confident in putting my best qualities forward.

I am always grateful for all that I am and all that I have.

I embrace all my amazing and unique qualities.

I see myself strong, happy, and content; my self-vision can become reality.

I can confidently feel the love I have for myself.

I know how to be humble whilst not compromising myself.

I respect myself and have a realistic acceptance of my own abilities and expectations; I am comfortable with the things that can't be changed.

I attract people and environments that support the person I am and my own personal universe.

I sometimes write or sketch to remember my five Ws and the H: who, what, when, where, why, and how.

I take time to stop, close my eyes, take a deep breath, and embrace my hopes and my dreams.

I create my own universe surrounded and supported by people, activities, and environments that support me, my happiness, and my contentment.

I know what I want to do; so what am I waiting for?

Keepsakes here

Printed in the United States
By Bookmasters